DISPLEASURES OF THE TABLE

BOOKS BY MARTHA RONK

Desire in L.A. (Athens: The University of Georgia Press, 1990)

Desert Geometries (Los Angeles: Littoral Books, 1992)

[with art by Don Suggs]

State of Mind (Los Angeles: Sun & Moon Press, 1995)

Eyetrouble (Athens: The University of Georgia Press, 1998)

Allegories (Italy: ML&NLF, 1998)

[with art by Tom Wudl, in Italian and English]

Displeasures of the Table

memoir as caricature

MARTHA RONK

GREEN INTEGER
KØBENHAVN
& LOS ANGELES
2001

GREEN INTEGER
Edited by Per Bregne
København/Los Angeles

Distributed in the United States by Consortium Book
Sales and Distribution, 1045 Westgate Drive, Suite 90
Saint Paul, Minnesota 55114-1065

(323) 857-1115 / http://www.greeninteger.com

10 9 8 7 6 5 4 3 2 1

Sections of this work were previously published in *Ribot*.

Publication of this book was made possible, in part,
through a matching grant from the California Arts Council.
This book was also published in collaboration with
The Contemporary Arts Educational Project, Inc.,
a non-profit corportation, through a matching grant from
the National Endowment for the Arts.

NATIONAL
ENDOWMENT
FOR ♥ THE
ARTS

Design: Per Bregne
Typography: Guy Bennett
Photograph: Photograph of Martha Ronk by Marcel Shaine

LIBRARY OF CONGRESS CATALOGING IN PUBLICATION DATA
Ronk, Martha [1940]
Displeasures of the Table
ISBN: 1-892295-44-X
p. cm — Green Integer
I. Title II. Series

Printed in Canada on acid-free paper.

For my sisters who remember everything differently, NANCY IHARA and PATRICIA FLUMENBAUM, and with thanks to PAUL VANGELISTI who assigned me a column on food for *Ribot* magazine where several of these pieces first appeared.

Contents

The dreadful and curious thing is that men, despoiled and having nothing, must long most for that which they have not and so, out of the intensity of their emptiness imagining they are full, deceive themselves and all the despoiled of the world into their sorry beliefs. It is the spirit that existing nowhere in them is forced into their dreams. The Pilgrims, they, the seed, instead of growing, looked black at the world and damning its perfections praised a zero in themselves.

— WILLIAM CARLOS WILLIAMS,
In The American Grain

TABLE
—*board, tablet, list*
—*to sit down to table, to eat*
—*under the table, not above board*

I don't sit still well and what character I have is restless if not melancholy. I don't much like eating or cooking either for that matter. Food itself is not exactly a displeasure; rather it may be I who am the Figure of

Displeasure hunched over a plate, although at my first tables rules took such precedence that I was generally squirmy. Or it may have been that I was simply meant to be a great sprinter.

Lately food has taken on such self-importance and such imported self-importance that again I want to leave tucked elbows and tucked napkins behind and tear through the streets faster and faster, vanishing into thin air. At age seven I thought I should be able to pass through houses as if they were transparent, though I was willing to strike a bargain and settle for a toe through the wall. These extremes, marked by abstinence and miracle, capture some of the oscillation bred into America and some Americans by Puritan heritage and adage. Waste not, want not. Try, try again. The earthly city or the heavenly one.

A is for Apple. Food as mnemonic device. We remember what we ate and who we might have been while eating an apple from a paper lunch sack. We use it to find out scenes lost in the past, recreated, pinned down by bookends, unreal finally as the food that allows us to loop back in time. I used to think I could remember books by eating them, that I could learn to read by mouthing the corners of pages which tasted of dust, glue, the ends of my own hair. I licked the page. I wanted to ingest all of Shakespeare's sonnets. What is it we *want* when we want to eat?

In this book I have tried to put eating and reading together, to come at them sideways. One odd consequence of time passing is that the memory of many years in which I thought I was making the most important decisions about life seem to have gone dim. Instead, I find childhood and yesterday clear and juxtaposed. There is no way anyhow to come at appetite head on. I began these "recipes" to get a glimpse of some version of a middle American past (albeit moved from Ohio to Connecticut to Los Angeles and Vermont) and a Protestant one of guilt and loneliness, lived, invented, let go, clung to. I have put eating and reading together as if one had to choose being in the world or not, wrestling with dough or syntax, being at the table or under it. What community I found was often in a book. *Sola Scriptura. Ars Poetica.*

I remember little of the events recounted here which once written seemed someone else's, someone's. Eating and writing as the inventions of the self. I remember little about my childhood past except in flashes of a street where I hung upside down from crabapple trees and rode a two wheeler with wooden blocks nailed to the pedals so I could reach the seat. It saved money to buy one bicycle, the one to grow into. It seems to me I spent hours lingering about and trying to get a grasp. I'm told I lived most of the time alone on a ledge behind the clothes in my closet, looking black at the world, talking to myself and being exaggeratedly sorry. I remain interested in being sorry and in what food it is for the soul, what self-indulgence perhaps, what compensation for forthrightness. I heard Julia Child on the radio say it was perfectly permissible to put marshmallows on Thanksgiving yams, pop them under the broiler for a few seconds to brown, so sweet. It was likewise so sweet and melting to be in the closet, as close as I've come to combining egotistic assertion and nonentity. It seems a neat trick, but perhaps not without its ill consequences.

Peas

Food in the form of princesses sleeping on twenty mattresses to find out, or what saints digest in their dreams. A wafer as thin as skin as the pea is hard. Some people have thin skins.

Some parents are accused of equating food with love; if it were only as easy as getting some chocolate, sprinkling it with chocolate and spreading it with a flat knife.

In the marketplace of ideas some prefer risotto which can also be served with peas for color. Which isn't to say this isn't a good idea or even an idea about cultures though not this one.

As a child growing up in Ohio, a place some equate with American simplicity and stupidity but which at the time I thought of as what is, I ate creamed peas and potatoes. I don't remember at all what this dish tasted like and I haven't had it since, but I do remember the shape of things in the mouth rolling around. Children today also seem to like frozen peas, how they stick together with small bits of ice and how they have to be pounded first to fit in the saucepan. My mother says I also ate fistfuls of sand from the sandbox. As I recall, an otherworldly experience. The best I have ever had were eaten raw standing in a row of peas in a garden in Readsboro, Vermont; they were also good cooked just then quickly in a bit of water with a bit of butter, but not so good.

In a movie in which the two are played as a couple, Dr. Watson doesn't want Holmes to interrupt him as he finishes eating his dinner which includes a few peas he is chasing around his plate; however, Holmes smashes them on a fork so they can get on with it. "Bloody rude, squashing a fellow's pea." My sympathies are with the detective. Eating seems, except for saints, a waste of time, or at least a hindrance to getting on with a vision or the ball. What either of those might be is a more difficult question.

A hard roll

For my mother the love of Benjamin Franklin and the love of self-improvement were one. I don't think she had a clue about his French amours. I don't think she kept ledgers either, but she did tally things up: report cards, posture, and cleanliness. In summer my sisters and I were sent out of doors in shorts and τ-shirts—no shoes—in imitation of Huck Finn. My mother wanted boys. In the days before parents planned each minute in the lives of their children, we were simply to go out and stay out digging channels in the mud until supper. The difference between the before and after line-ups was therefore dramatic.

We were given laundry detergent and scrub brushes for our elbows and knees and paraded downstairs for inspection. My father wore only white shirts to work and taught me to fold his pocket handkerchief in tight triangles. I had ironed them or sent them through the mangle until they were smooth as the sheets. He looked at himself in the bathroom mirror and tried with tweezers to improve on what he saw.

At first Benjamin Franklin enters Philadelphia dirty and poor, a hard roll under each arm. Balzac said of him that he invented the lightning rod, the hoax (*le canard*) and the republic. Also self-improvement, both the ordinary and the profound. On TV talk shows awkward young women stumble forward in ill-fitting shoes and after a time behind the curtain they return to the applause of the studio audience with hair coifed, lipstick applied, and nails done. I see transformation all around me. I'm skeptical, but only somewhat. One mocks optimism at some cost and often at the cost of someone different from oneself. And also I like one hard roll.

Goose liver pâté

What I mean when I say that I think Americans are not really materialists is that food substitutes for idea, idea for food.

The idea of goose liver pâté as merely the first of many courses leaves me feeling stuffed and greenish not to mention the actual liver-shaped and liver-colored thing itself. Once I had a skin-tight bile green sweater but that's another story. It's too palpitating, too over-wrought. Pâté is status. For my parents status was else-where; guests on the screen porch ate simple stew out of paper bowls and drank expensive scotch. The op-erative idea was the idea of picnic, a picnic was leisure and privilege. As a child it seems easy to attach to the physical world; it is close by and easily at hand. One teacher I know takes her class to a park to play with popsicle sticks in the mud.

Peanutbutter sandwiches

Say peanutbutter over and over.
Say you use ordinary language and eat ordinary food.
Say you say it over and over until it's something else.
Say it isn't so.
Sez *is what Uncle Ez says.*
To say uncle.

My uncle was named Earl and married to Aunt Pearl
and lived in Sandusky in a green house by the rail-
road tracks. Even as a child I knew this chiming of
names was improbable. Since it was a second marriage I thought they had taken them with their vows
as proof of legitimacy. At night the train went through
the bedroom I slept in, across the pillow, the ceiling,
the dream I was having and my sister's scream. They
decorated the tiny house in Chinoiserie and kept stacks
of old newspapers in the basement so I could cut out
the Sunday Tillie Dolls and all their clothes and think
up a new life. The mantel was crammed with statues
of girls in pink bonnets, ceramic ribbons flying. They
drove a lavender cadillac with black and gold uphol-
stery and fins that thrust into the very seat of passion.

Isn't it the most beautiful car in the world I said to my mother. Pearl had pearlwhite hair, all fake my mother said, and she had chosen the wallpaper for the Lady's Room at the Yacht Club; it had red flocking on wide roses. I rubbed my hands across it, splashed on the free and cheap cologne.

When I was an au pair girl in Germany I tried to make an American lunch for my family and put raw peanuts in a blender. No one could see the point once I had made my presentation with the crusts cut off and neither could I. America seemed so far away, unformed and new. But I had to go home eventually and I returned to my love of peanutbutter sandwiches and ordinary language for conveying ordinary things. My uncle used to sneak up behind us and knead our kneecaps and cry, "I'll break every bone in your body," my first encounter with rhetoric.

Lake Erie perch

The Merry-Go-Round at Put-In-Bay still had animals not just horses: pigs and goats and a rooster with a red cockscomb so slippery I clung to it as I rode into dizziness. We ate perch at a long table in a restaurant near the lake, but I only remember the bones and a terror of the unexpected so deftly planted in this fish. There was no way to tell when you'd come across one which would poke and stick and eventually lodge in your throat and you'd choke and die.

Anticipation is the worst. It isn't so bad once you get on the airplane but ahead of time I want to see everyone I've ever known and phone up those I love. It's the image of the stewardess plunging through the air, her clothes unraveling across the great plains. In the Lake Erie boathouse there hung a sign: Am I My Brother's Keeper? One of the brothers was a minister and preached the same sermon every summer about grace pouring from a pitcher in the sky. The sky was vastly blue with white clouds and suspended up there—no trick wires—was the pewter pitcher we used to water houseplants, large and improbable, a slate colored *objet d'art*. Surrealism in a pew. A man I know went with his parents to church in San Francisco. The mass in Latin when he was young, was then in Italian, then English, now Chinese. Almost as good as Latin, he says.

I wasn't afraid of the water and we plunged in and out of Lake Erie and took on waves and were thrown great distances from my father's shoulders. Myopic and waterlogged, I saw the world in a blur: people normally separate and intact joined together at the hips, faces erased, my sister's feet grew out from the center of my father's chest, her arms fluttering in a triangle against the sky before she dove and disappeared.

The boat was called No Name III, a fact that worried me, not only nothingness itself which was hard enough, but nothingness to the third power. I knew shapes shifted and oozed but it was trying to think of "not being" as one clung to the sides of the boat.

Bread for dessert

This is a good thing to serve because you don't have to bake it or sift it or measure it. You just go out to a bakery somewhere and buy a good loaf and slice it. Some say it soaks up the alcohol so you can drive home which in L.A. is always a longer distance than you think even if you close one eye. If you want you can use butter or olive oil with a few rosemary leaves in it. I can't grow anything, but my rosemary plant seems to thrive. Some things, like grace or sudden ease, just do thrive better without fret.

When I was a child in Ohio we were given Wonder Bread with butter and sugar for dessert. I don't know why mother relented in this extravagant way, except that it was cheap. Usually white sugar was as forbidden as leaving for church without white gloves. My father sent me back for them every time and every time I tried to hide the soiled fingers by folding them over slightly. I was supposed to wash them in between Sundays but the week went by so quickly. What I remember is the odd feeling of washing gloves on one's

24

hands, like a second skin, like what it would be like sleeping in the same bed with someone else.

Afternoons, hot and sticky and August, I'd get a pile of books from the brick library and sit in the screened-in porch and read until dinnertime. It was too hot to move. Because I wasn't to eat between meals, I'd have to sneak in for a slice of bread from the bread box with the strawberry decal on the front. I'd pinch off a little piece and ball it up in my palms until it was a sticky little mass, slightly gray. No bread has ever been as good as reading *A Horse of Her Own* over and over like this.

Corn

Across the way Mr. Parsons filled the vacant lot with corn. In August he came over with arms full and when he and his family went on vacation we could go every early evening and pick ears for dinner. The shucking took place in the narrow strip of back yard as we, my sisters and mother and I, sat on plastic lawn chairs, shifting in our shorts as the webbing stuck, and talking. Our cat Gypsy who had wandered in from nowhere and lived 20 years and produced litters of kittens also loved corn and would eat it from end to end and then turn the cob with her paw to begin on the next row. After a dinner of corn, we'd return to the backyard and watch her do it until the fireflies came out. We'd talk to put off bedtime, we'd talk as if it could be put off past time itself, that talk could take its place.

Later a house went in where the corn had been. The Parsons moved and we grew up. It never occurred to me then that having someone to listen to one's chatter was as unusual as finding corn across the way in a city. As one grows up one loses the perfect audience or it shifts from family to those who think as one does or work as one does or write as one does. Someone says *yes* to one's sense of feeling (Sartre says so in *The Words*) artificial most of the time. One holds the receiver; the dizzying shift of most of the time holds still for a moment. Most poets I know have given up on audience; it is in the future, they say; it is oneself; it is irrelevant; who cares. I give up on corn; it will never taste the same.

Brussels sprouts

The Protestants outdid the medieval preachers in denouncing innate depravity. The thing itself was not merely for them a poor bare, forked animal; it was a sink of iniquity. They diagnosed mankind as "accursed, poisonous, ruinating, dismall, Woefull, Miserable, and forlorn...."

—SACVAN BERCOVITCH,
The Puritan Origins of the American Self

To take it, to have the wind knocked out, to swallow it whole, to know one's place. We had to eat everything on our plates. Mother took us to the downtown church so we would know the rich and the poor. The Armenians were starving. Or else you sat there alone in gray twilight listening to the distant sounds of playing after dinner and facing five lumps of brussels sprouts on a plate. I know them now as ranged bulbs on a thick stem, a trident, magical and bright as modern lamps with swivel heads to ward off the dark. But then they were soggy with defrosting and boiling and sat in a tasteless row. Let me go, I'd insist, go away. But like arguments into the night when the other party won't quit, but keeps worrying the knot, there they sat. Exhausted by fury, an emotion more tiring for the

28

sheer inexplicability of it, its takeover of heartbeat and limbs, I sat. Injustice and reverie descended in a sodden mass upon me and I knew myself adopted, forlorn, exiled.

Some like Elizabeth Bishop went to other countries to find poetry, Paris, a woman to love. Some were exiled at home by prejudice and a cardboard sign worn to school that said, "I don't speak English." By what rights did I, small and inarticulate, sitting with my brussels sprouts, imagine that I was of their company. Gone off to no war, adrift on no sea, called to nothing but repentance.

I take a deep breath. I swallow each sprout whole. I am rebaptized into the human race. I put body behind me and run into a world of grassy light.

Cherries

Today, unlike yesterday, memory is missing from my mouth. It used to be that I didn't know I was hungry until in the middle of the afternoon I'd get a headache and those little bright lights in front of my eyes and I'd find myself wandering around among racks of dresses in some department store after a bad session with a therapist and it would occur to me. Rhapsody over a cherry pie stimulates amnesia. One can forget almost anything with that red sweetness melting in the mouth. In *Twelfth Night*, Toby, the promoter of cakes and ale, sings, "I will never die."

I think it's that sweets come round with mechanical regularity and take one's mind off the black cloud floating overhead which, like Joe Btfsplk, is something I do take for granted. I never made a cherry pie or tart or anything, but once I helped pick cherries off a tree, the juice running down my outstretched arms, my mind turned off.

My father always said, life is just a bowl of cherries. After dance recitals he would always say, ok but you've got to learn to smile.

Beautiful soup

Doesn't it seem that memory comes in black and white? I don't mean that I can't remember that my mother's best dress was blue with wavy lines running through it, a dress she had tailored for her in a gesture of extravagance I hoped dearly to inherit, but didn't. Perhaps my father's extravagance directed only at her kept the line short and pure: pearl earrings one birthday so heavy and gleaming she went right out, against all scruples and had her ears pierced. I read that children hate the doctor's needle because they think they'll leak from the tiny hole.

I, however, inherited a tendency towards plainness as did many I knew, the serious girls in grade school and beyond. No one I knew wore Fire and Ice nail polish though my mother did. No one put on rhinestones and danced far into the night. No one wore Shalimar.

I remember as children we stayed put, sipping Campbell's soup and reading comics at the kitchen table arguing over quadrants of table space as our parents, the grand ones, dressed in tails and satin, and slipped out into the night. I still am reading at table and still prefer soup from a can. I know I must be wrong; I can't seem to help it. The lines of print are so beautifully black and white. The black and white photograph of my grandmother hangs on the wall, her mouth severe. She's lost in thought.

Chocolate turtles

Desires were to be squashed. Down Satan down.
Whenever something took over, and I believe that is
how I thought of it—being possessed in some way
that caused a coursing in the veins, a headachey throb
between the ears, a tumult in the stomach—I was sent
outside to ride my bike madly until it passed. I wanted
too much, I had tilted the house. Someone wanted to
pick me up like a ragdoll and throw me against the
wall or I wanted someone to. I wept, I flailed, I bur-
rowed in stories of the maligned and abandoned.

For Father's Day I decided that my father should get a
box of turtles which I bought at Eagle's Candy Shop
up Andover Road and left past the apartments where
my best friend's grandparents sat in dark rooms. The
candy came in white cardboard boxes like boxes for
men's shirts only smaller with slots and flaps that fit
together ingeniously. I sped along on my bike spreading my arms out wide like a great bird or jumping
curbs until whatever it was had taken me would slowly
drain away and I'd feel back to some semblance again,
neat and plaid.

A woman I talked long hours with mentioned the plaid dresses with white collars we used to wear; what I remembered as she talked was liking them until the cotton front no longer lay flat. The turtles were assorted, dark or milk chocolate over nuts. With coffee after dinner my father had these on special occasions or one thin mint or maybe two for dessert. On his birthday he lowered a spoonful of lighted brandy into the coffeecup and the whole surface turned an oily pool of fire to dive into from great and daring heights if only one weren't so big, so ungainly, so huge. I didn't covet the turtles.

What I wanted was to work in an office downtown; I wanted my father's brown suit and lace up shoes; I wanted not to cook dinner for anyone; I wanted to speed through the world to Poughkeepsie. I wanted all the time—not something sweet and chocolate, not the yellow dress with velvet ribbons my mother said wasn't right, not dance camp with the older girls. I wanted tumult until my stomach hurt and ulcers a bit later on.

Raisins

Eyes for the most part. In one cartoon the mother points out the faces all over the house, the knobs and spigot in the washbowl, the windows and door on the front, the two evenly hung pictures above the open mouth of the fireplace, and the child freaks. There is the gingercookie cut to the shape of a man or with skirt to a woman and it is inanimate as all get out until you get the two raisins poked in. A child develops to another Piaget level when she learns to pencil in the eyes and put finger marks at the ends of the sticks. Self-consciousness goes with the territory; on the American plains we are little dots in the vast distance, not grouped together in the plaza, and we take it for granted. Sundays we imagine ourselves on the green field, our eye on the ball, all eyes on us, heroic and alone.

A Dagwood sandwich

In the Sunday comics the printing was always a bit off register, the colors just beyond the hard outline of a character like Dagwood, his yellow shirt bleeding onto the couch he is sleeping on. The salami brown in his sandwich hangs over the edge. This was a sign of something, I didn't know what, but I knew it was a sign. Everything was meaningful, you just had to plumb it and find it out. I try to think where this idea came from. Perhaps from the King James version of the Bible, a text in difficult if seductive language. Perhaps from the absolute rift my parents set up between the world of adults and the world of children so that rules that seemed arbitrary weren't, but you couldn't quite see why. Perhaps it was that I thought too much which is what my mother said to me, you think too much.

More important to me even than the overlapping of color and line was that certain words were printed in bold letters. I was certain it was a message from elsewhere, another world trying to get in and I was the chosen decoder, the one who could piece it together by linking up the black letters. I knew if one could just learn to read the world aright one would know some mystery as yet unidentified.

What did I think I'd know? At this distance I'm not at all sure. I remember an overwhelming and simultaneous feeling of urgency and certitude. I remember hours with the newspaper spread open on the floor in front of me as I wrote down variations and combinations. Perhaps it was the divine I was after or perhaps it was something closer to hand such as why I had to take care of my sisters. I knew I would fail and be damned, not only because I pushed them off the front stoop, but because I couldn't figure out the meaning of things.

Things stand for what they are seems a simple enough truth but I couldn't get it. It ought somehow to have had to do with sex, but it didn't. It came from the printing press, from a man who moved a roller just a tad to the left, botching the register, and then left his office in the middle of the night and vanished like so much else.

Milk

I spent my childhood knocking glasses of it onto the blue rug under the dining room table. I don't think I meant to although as I think back on it I might have. It was perhaps an inarticulate protest at the multitudes of rules: knees together, straight A's, cropped hair, sensible shoes, Saturday chores: raking the leaves, sweeping the garage, dusting the moldings.

I crept around the room moving the rag from the ragbag along the narrow ridge for what seemed endless hours on a sunny day. The day funneled in to a beam of light filled with dust motes, to the inch just in front of the rag, to the endlessness of the task which once over would soon come again. I remember being all knees, one knee after another knee after another knee and the slight skin burn from the rug. Kneeling in church made me faint, rising and falling on the verge of blacking out just before the "devices and desires" part of the Confession.

And I didn't want to spill my milk or to disappoint one more time; I was mortified to be on my knees between all those legs and shoes mopping up the sour smell with a damp rag. Is there anything to be made of such small mortifications? What would it mean to grow up without them, without the relief of self-loathing, without the stiffening of the spine?

Milktoast

When I was sick as a child the cures were ritual reassurances. My mother wrapped a camphor-drenched sock of my father's around my throat and plugged in a steam thing that looked like the spout on a tugboat. Draped in a towel it looked like a terrycloth guardian that made a faint wheezing sound I imitated under the sheets until I was asleep. She gave me teaspoons of lemon, honey, whiskey in various strengths at timed intervals throughout the night and day. She had me lie in bed and listen to hours of radio drama which filled my already feverish mind with dreams of small town romance I have not yet recovered from. She let me act out the radio dramas with paperdolls cut from the newspaper which I dressed in ways she would have called seductive and which kept my own sexual fantasies carefully put away in envelopes at the end of the day.

For dinner I got milktoast, buttered toast at the bottom of a shallow bowl drowned in warm milk. You eat it with a soup spoon. Someone comes and then leaves the room. You eat in a hush.

Food has always been ritual, never more so than in the face of sickness. Can it be accident that the sign I saw yesterday in Koreatown said "Mom's Donuts and Chinese Take Out"—the stylized mom's face lifted from Life Magazine circa 1954?

Balsamic vinegar

Life is a train of moods like a string of beads, and as we pass through them they prove to be many-colored lenses which paint the world their own hue, and each shows only what lies in its focus. From the mountain you see only the mountain. We animate what we can, and we see only what we animate.

What Emerson says isn't, as has been wrongly reported to me, that we should rush around gathering more and more experience in a fit of frenzy. This is not to say that we haven't behaved in just this way, rushing here and there on errands, fixing things up, putting in rheostats and trying to see all there is to see. Since I've always gone in for rushing, the rhyme about the bear was recited to me as an object lesson: *The bear went over the mountain, the bear went over the mountain, the bear went over the mountain to see what he could see. The other side of the mountain, the other side of the mountain, the other side of the mountain, is all that he could see.*

Which is what is often wrong with meals. There are too many parts and too many directions so that having finished the tomatoes my sister grew, large and red and dressed, one is faced with a meat course and vegetables and all sorts of pasta and bread and desert, goat cheese melting. Our cities are built for rushing and not much else. There is nothing to look at except the freeway one is traveling on to get to the next. One course is barely cleared away before another appears. Before such distraction, the bite of balsamic lingers on the tongue, the sweet sadness of something that pricks us where we bleed.

Hash

There were so many things in which one could get fingers caught, screens and car doors slamming and the rubber fan my mother was afraid we'd cut our fingers off it was so rubbery and slow the air barely turned and of course the mangle which offered up the temptation to dive into the steam and white sheets and just let both hands flatten under the turning roller, a whole long body in tow and done in down in the basement while the rest of the world went on and didn't know we'd been flattened like paper. The fan was ugly and thick and smelled of ether. The mangle a sort of sleep machine. The hash machine you pushed wet carrots and slippery chunks of meat and potato from the potroast left over from last night through and was it my sister turning the handle as I pushed and watched it come out the metal nose cone as the hash we'd have for dinner. You could lose a finger there or in the spokes of the bicycle or if in defiance you rode around barefoot and dangled your feet you could catch them and slice off your toes as you rounded the corner to glide into the plains singing cowboy songs and learning to yodel.

Lima beans

My mother preferred frozen lima beans when the ease of the freezer and Bird's Eye had captured the nation. Later, for unknown reasons, she abandoned the frozen ones and took up dried lima beans for Christmas eve dinner. They had a kind of overcooked and undercooked consistency, a cardboard chewiness which made one aware of a plant's cellular structure. They were served as the sole course, her idea I think of fasting or of the seasonal triumph of turning a dried bean into food. I knew this as idea and was interested in it as idea, but like so many other rituals of my childhood, I was unable to ask the right question or the answer was buried somewhere even my mother didn't know.

Afterwards we would all pile in the car and drive slowly around the neighborhood to look at the houses lit up and would ooh and aah and clap. I made cutout figures for a felt board performance with baby Jesus and elves and Santa Claus and made everyone watch while I assumed different high-pitched voices, my idea of the theatrical. I know this as nostalgia. I knew it even then.

The five of us were making memories, not exactly having a good holiday, but constructing what it would be at some future time. My father got out the 8mm camera and we were directed to walk down the stairs with appropriate expressions of surprise as the tree came into view. If the camera jammed, as it always did, we went to the top of the stairs and did it again.

Christmas cookies

By accident Christmas is associated in my mind with
Australia, a country I've never been to and never will.
By accident a kangaroo got in with the other cookie
cutters, the usual stars and bells and trees, in the back
of the kitchen drawer. It was hard to handle; the sticky
dough caught and it came out pathetically as a tailless
lizardy sort of thing. We always made rollout cookies
cut into shapes and decorated. In the German man-
ner the cookie sheet was covered with anise seeds and
after the baking the cookies were spread with white
icing and sprinkled with green and red colored sugar.
The seven minute sugar icing cooked in the top of a
double boiler and the kitchen smelled of steam and
sugar as the icing was got on quickly before it hard-
ened into crystals and stuck to the sides of the pan.

What to do about adjectives perplexes many a writer I
know. Others reject them outright, altogether, and always; others pile them up as if the ornate prose of the
last century could be maintained by will power and
skill. The Christmas cookies were clearly too rich and
gooey and these days I make them plain or no one

will eat them at all. For years I refused Hemingway, but I no longer do. I'll never go where he goes; like Australia it's too far. Where one lives and what one makes is only partly choice, but it's also partly random and happenstance, a particular cookie cutter in a particular kitchen drawer.

Green beans

Thoreau's may not have been green, but for me the best are. Or purplish mottled from last summer or long pole beans hanging down like fingers next to the upright bamboo, your own lacing with them as you pick next to the rubbery vines unable to tell where one thing stops and another begins. You can look at a bush bean for a long time before one comes out of the green into focus, clumped usually with several others. "It was no longer beans that I hoed, nor I that hoed beans." He says he learned economy and transcendence. Metaphor in Thoreau stands there and stands out.

Some poets have taken recently to excising metaphor: it has no place and connection is a fake. "Trace the gold sun about the whitened sky/ Without evasion by a single metaphor" (Wallace Stevens) I stand on this question as I often stand on far more questions than I would wish, on the fence. Both positions seem to avoid an essential tension, and I, Janus addict that I am, prefer having to look in two directions at once, having to jostle against one thing and another, having to modify response, having to go back over the same ground.

Setting things side by side can be stolid and obvious, but it can also open up and unsettle, even in trace or negative form.

It is Vermont August and the sunny days tilt towards July, the nights towards September. I am finally and completely at home in my cabin; I am in tears all day and for no reason. I find it so inexplicable as to be not only without cause, but without person. I look around to see who is so overwrought. Even seasons of beans are not clear-cut. At its best metaphor operates as complexly as the Roman god of open doors, gates, and all other beginnings.

Lemons 1

I would like to make poems out of real objects. The lemon to be a lemon that the reader could cut or squeeze or taste...Things do not connect; they correspond. That is what makes it possible for a poet to translate real objects, to bring them across language as easily as he can bring them across time.

—JACK SPICER

There is no such thing as a real lemon. If you punch holes in several with an ice pick you can stick them in the cavity of a chicken and tie its legs together and flavor the whole which also, if you are lucky, puffs up as you carry it to the table, but deflates immediately as you remove it from the oven. Nevertheless, it's a good show. Obviously also salt and pepper. There may, however, be correspondence. This is tricky, especially for those of us from Ohio who have allegorical temperaments. The lemon is as much like Ophelia as anything else (her opening letter) as the opposite or boys in blue bathing suits which Spicer liked quite well. Images have been under attack since the Puritans labeled them seductive; lop the nose off they said, rip the canvas. My lemon sits in wedges, her skirts are yellow as all get out and her correspondence always begins, dearest love, how are you?

Lemons 2

The amount of distance between the thing and the word varies greatly for different folks. Bucyrus, for example, ought to have been covered in Byzantine mosaic I thought as a child as we passed through it on the way to Sandusky and as I rolled the sound of it around in my mouth, but it wasn't. Once there we did, however, eat the best blueberry muffins I've ever eaten, the berries like bits of blue shine. I didn't like having a purple tongue though I liked sticking it out at those who weren't looking.

It is not a question so much of whether or not there is a real blueberry or lemon but how and why it gets into the poem. Insistence upon the senses pleases those who also believe paychecks will make them happy. We got to Bucyrus on Route 40. I was always carsick. The so-called real lemon is no more so than the so-called allegorical one; it depends on what it's doing on one's plate.

Eating it doesn't make it real, nor its symbolic freight: the ochre of old age, the sunny giddiness of childhood, the *memento mori* of still life lemons curling and turning blue with mold. Nor the proliferation of adjectives and emotions as the man presses his torn and dirty fingernail into the lemon, leering and sprouting chest hairs as he does. "Fails to meet one's expectations; drives off in, the exhaust pipe dragging," *American Heritage.*

Nor the boundless desire to meet over an agreed-upon lemon tart once made for me in San Francisco after a poetry reading both of which elicited a variety of response. *Give me the recipe* is always one. *Don't explain* is another and also a song I heard years after Bucyrus when I was in love because of it. What gets left out if one squeezes the lemon; what gets left out if one doesn't? At least poets need to address lemons; most others can be invited later for martinis which can be served also with olives.

Spinach and self-reliance

Talking about food is what many people like to do. My first experience of this was when I was visiting the family of the man I married. We were eating a leg of lamb, but no one paid much mind to what was on the serving dish but rather to a transcendent leg of lamb my prospective father-in-law had eaten many years before. He was a scientist and not usually rhapsodic yet here he was going on and on about heavenly texture and something that floated like a great pink Degas thigh out of the past and over the table-cloth. No one noticed the whites of my rolling eyes. At my house no one spoke of politics, sex, or food.

Since that time, I have encountered others who talk about cups of coffee, soups and stews. Last night a woman who is the most sturdy of the sensitive souls I tender great affection for, said that she poses formal questions to her children at table: what did you do at school today, and what experience did you have that caused you most thought? Now here are good topics for conversation, I thought—serious and self-improving.

Her children, however, refuse these obvious ploys and eat. Later they will no doubt take up the communal habit of talking about their mother's cooking; even I remember the steaming rice balls she made in the kitchen of their house in Japan. My favorite food is spinach because it tends towards watery evaporation and no one seems to have any stories about it.

Mashed potato patties

Leftovers were staples. Now we steal quotations and pad out poems. Sometimes I can't even remember where they came from. Recently, I stole a quotation which I had once taken from somewhere but now can't remember: "A face which inspires fear or delight not its cause, one might say, its target." I keep catching on the word "it" as a skirt catches on the nail not quite pounded in. And that face, Sienese perhaps, haunting and haloed in gold gilt. Or the other faces, not the ones we love, but the faces that drag us after them through street after street. Or the portrait with eyes that ought to be dead as paint, but aren't.

It's impossible to steal one's own image or even see it really except once in a while in a store window or in the photograph of a photographer reflected in a store window. Once I took a picture of myself in a mirror in a convent in Rome. It was siesta but I couldn't sleep for the terrible heat. There is a crucifix on the wall beside the mirror but nothing else of the city—no Forum or Coliseum or St. Ivo. But when I look at it I see the city in that hot August and I feel the bottoms of my feet in dusty sandals walking around the Baths of Caracalla. The outside of these fried patties was crispy; the inside the melt of mashed potato. Unlike other leftovers we had them rarely since mashed potatoes themselves were for holidays. It is not so easy to find the right quote and tempting to use just any old one.

Grapes

A mouth of liquid celadon, children's hands pulling them off the stem one by one by one. It pleases them to eat in orderly sequence, food so often messy and glopped together, so all of a piece in abominable casserole. The juices of one run into the juices of another and the children scream as if they'd seen an alien, the conquest of the planet at hand. But these contribute to the mastery of language, each word separated off from the garble of *before*, the confusion of *after*.

Yoghurt

I like yoghurt in small cardboard containers, also formal poems, especially sonnets. Most everyone I know likes process art and the unedited, run-together details of daybooks or lists. The vanilla is cold and as easy as babyfood and nostalgia. The shape of the spoon is as delicious as if it were silver and one could eat color. Someone I know uses Gerber jars to store pieces of Death Valley, the green looks like peas, the yellow like squash, the whole of the desert in a jar with the lid screwed on. That's my idea of heavenly pie.

But if you take instant vanilla pudding and add chocolate chips and put the mixture in a graham cracker crust and cover the whole with gobs of whipped cream you'll have what I had for every birthday party until I was twelve. Then I was so romantic I draped my scrawny frame in gauze and imagined I could dance Giselle. There is a photograph of it somewhere.

Cereal

Cereal as the bowl of the ordinary is what many have for breakfast and it insists on remaining ordinary no matter what athletes say. You just dump some flakes into a bowl and add milk, or if you are my nephew, apple juice. Even hot cereals take only a little more time and cleaning the pot afterwards. My son used to come home from school and no matter what else was in the refrigerator, dump Cheerios into a bowl, and hunker down silent over *The Silver Surfer,* avoiding the inevitable. He always beat me at 20 questions by using a super hero as what he was thinking of. My mother says that when I was little I sat on the steps of the apartment building in Cleveland eating cheerios out of a tin cup and offering them to strangers. I think most conversations occur on steps, either with imaginary friends or with those who are passing up or down. Perhaps it's the awkwardness of the steps, the teeter of the feet, the noncommittal shift of weight. I used to talk to Linda who, my mother told me, wasn't real. I remember her patent leather shoes, the plaid ribbons on her braids, her papery face.

Now as I wash the dishes alone, no one in the house and no one about to arrive, I am surrounded by with absent friends and lovers; they stand close about me ghostly, vivid. Someone on the stairs hands me a xerox from his beloved Emily Dickinson:

> A charm invests a face
> Imperfectly beheld,—
> The lady dare not lift her veil
> For fear it be dispelled.
>
> But peers beyond her mesh,
> And wishes, and denies,—
> Lest interview annul a want
> That image satisfies.

Boiling water

What most people seem to like about food is what I find most taxing, metaphysically speaking. It is so transitory. One has to keep after it, keep bringing groceries into the kitchen, sorting through brown bags, going to markets, boiling the water, eating and then finding that it is time to eat again and then going to the refrigerator to get more and finding that one is out and also that there is no way to store up ahead of time so that you can keep on working and not get hungry. The little light spots in front of the eyes keep coming on. Of course it is like death. Of course I thought at age nine, anyone would choose poetry I loved it from the get-go because it had been written so long ago, because as Shakespeare insists, it lasts longer than gilded monuments, because the voices are still around first on the page and then in the head, because the fragments of Sappho attach themselves to us like damp feathers.

> *For a moment she rested against me*
> *Like a swallow half blown to the wall.*
> —EZRA POUND

Frozen hotdogs

Simple Simon met a pieman or Jack Horner stuck in his thumb or the man who was wondrous wise jumped into a bramble bush and scratched out both his eyes—

> *And then because his eyes were out*
> *With all his might and main*
> *He jumped into a bramble bush*
> *And scratched them in again.*

Such rhymes stamped themselves on what I thought of as my lesser mind which, like the box of treasures in the upper reaches of my closet (odd bits of cloth, an as-yet-unironed ribbon), held memory and the logic of the man who had figured out how to get his eyes back.

A table companion and I talked about clothes in the backs of our closets, a blouse way too small, a prom skirt I recently had repaired for no good reason, a Mod Mini too short to sit down in even then. Like my mother's going-away-dress, they fall into rags and the rags folded into a drawer under the bed to be come across each spring. Nursery rhymes declared the lunacy of the world: sottish, silly, muddy.

Down the street on Five Mile River Road lived the Hall Family. I was asked to babysit; my mother warned of the mess. Was it because Mrs. Hall was British, I wondered, was that it. I arrived just as they were to leave, the kitchen table spread with bolts of muslin, Mrs. Hall in a slip, her evening dress under one arm, was stamping messy flower decals on the edges of what might be curtains she explained they were having such a good time and time had got away from them and it had been a rainy day so good for long projects didn't I think and she had ink all over her hands and hadn't a chance to feed the boys would I find something, anything, surely there must be frozen hotdogs to boil up or something in the fridge and it was past their bedtime and if I could find their pajamas would I mind finding them and I could leave everything as is and by that time she had got her arms into a heavily beaded dress and was out the door with Mr. Hall and a comb. The boys took two or three hotdogs from the plastic and said they liked them icy. They said they'd done the prints on the left side and showed me, their eyes wide, their fingernails blue. I could only do what I knew how to do. I recited the nursery rhymes I knew by heart and put them in bed and washed up pots left for what must have been days soaking in the sink. It turns out there is some sort of point in keeping dresses that get smaller and more threadbare each year. Some things are what they are because they are beside the point.

Creamed tunafish on toast

As a college student I was to make dinner for a college minister. Even now I am embarrassed by the fact that, although I remember clearly that we were poor, I made glutinous creamed tunafish on toast which several other students and I ate with him on the lawn in front of Sterling Chapel in New Haven. In the house I grew up in, one day a week, usually a Monday, we had a money-saving meal: creamed tuna, creamed hard-boiled eggs, creamed chipped beef, all on white toast.

The minister and his wife didn't eat I don't think; they were gracious in ways I couldn't then see. I was young. I hated grace. I hated religion. He climbed the belltower and we all sat leaning on our palms in the grass watching as if it were and were not happening as the sun went down. It had the stillness of going on and on, as we watched him inch his way up, not only because it took so much time, but also because it was so potently and embarrassingly symbolic. The grass was August brown and warm.

The problem with syntax is that it is so demanding, demanding of explanation, of meaningful connection between the past and present, of causality and drama, of art and belief. The problem with giving it up altogether, as much contemporary writing does, is that it asks us to take that which is missing on faith, as if it were more complex and compelling because unsaid. What I've always wanted was someone to love me who could simply read my mind.

Pasta

Everybody's eating it. We used to have spaghetti, but no more, now we have pasta and arguments over homemade, DeCecco, Martelli, the number of minutes and how just eleven, not twelve as it says on the package, is perfect (or more in lower altitudes), but you have to stand over the boiling water and keep tasting to be perfectly sure. Once I arrived for dinner in Cambridge, Mass. and the cook had made pasta and cut it and it was drying it over all the kitchen chairs like winter socks, too beautiful to eat.

There was one Italian restaurant in town when I was growing up and on special occasions or when my father was out of town on business, we went there, my mother in stockings, three girls in white socks. This is when there were still meatballs with the spaghetti and the grated cheese came in glass containers with a screw-on lid and a jointed flap, not with a waiter and a grater. I have no idea whether the food was any good; I only remember silliness, the silliness of the girls' night out and the lapse of father's law, in which the timeless cocoon of my mother was all ours—all perfume and swinging of legs under table and pinching of skin and flipping of hair and giggling so hard not one of us could spin the fork in the spoon.

And at my back I always hear/ Time's winged chariot drawing near, a line that now belongs as much to Eliot's *Wasteland* as to Andrew Marvell. The high seriousness of the culture of pasta is the opposite of silliness. Like the egg races we used to have running for dear life across the playing field with a live egg balanced on a spoon.

Lobster

To abandon human standards; someone said this is what Emily Bronte knew. (*My sister Emily loved the moor....She found in the bleak solitude many and dear delights.*) It is a question of how much of it one can take and why one takes it. Someone said that how one feels about eating is how one feels about life and I myself have certainly said of one who likes to eat, cook, and talk food: he loves life.

Yet it depends, of course, on what life is; and the nature of the human; and where one stands to view it. Giving up as in Lenten practice or swooning surrender is as close to life as the mounds of lobster the same man, a former monk, told me—in a tone of mock shock—were heaped up high on Good Friday. You'd come into the refectory from evensong and there they'd be, boiled and red, for the calendar day of fasting. Once I bought a used Toyota that never ran; as long as it's not red I told the salesman. I did once buy a red tent dress for a wedding because the model who took me shopping said I had to, "it's so you." It was stunning she said, and I felt as fashion-able as I've ever felt, as distant from any life I had had or would ever have.

Peanuts

My father had cocktails before dinner and read the paper.

It sounds to me rereading that sentence as if I were born in the last century surrounded by pipesmoke and heavy woolen suits that had to be aired out on the line. He ate Spanish nuts with his cocktail; they fell out of a sort of drawer at the bottom of a plastic Mr. Peanuts contraption that Aunt Nadine had sent perhaps as a joke from Cleveland. Imagination was measured in those days by a taste in oddities: an old fashioned ceramic telephone with red roses, a "plant" made of plastic glowthings on the table in the front hallway. I made an apple turkey for the Thanksgiving table, four toothpicks for the feet, a concession to balance over reality, and pipecleaner pilgrims which would never stand no matter what you did to their feet.

The peanuts were meant only for my father; children were to disappear during cocktail hour, be neither seen nor heard. You snuck around from behind, pushed a lever, and an exact amount fell into your hand. I loved the moment of measure. It was a thrill. I imagined a future in which I wore only very spiked high-heeled shoes.

Oranges

The worst color for lipstick is orange; also it's like kissing when you are twelve and you don't much see the point. Oranges are like large monkeys when you begin to read and come to what O is for. I can't remember learning to read only relief at something finally to do that seemed as important as running or riding my bike. Didn't you ever date a football player a man from Texas asked at dinner last night as I tried to describe what I thought was the smell of fear. For a long time I had a memory box to keep treasures in as if the things themselves would bring back time; in there was a gold football on a chain. If you peel an orange with your thumb without breaking the curl of the rind, something good will happen to you and if you throw the curl of apple peel over your left shoulder, you will find out the first initial of the one you will marry. At the same time as I remember licking my lips until they were chapped summer and winter, mother discovered that if she transferred the frozen orange juice from the freezer to the refrigerator before she went to bed, by morning it would be thawed enough just to add water and stir.

Grains

One afternoon when I was still sixteen I was called to the bedroom of my boyfriend's mother who had a separate bedroom and a prodigious appetite. The family had moved from Iowa and all of them ate as if food could replace displacement. This was a problem of promotion. Men, mildly successful in grains, were sent east and suffered for the rest of their lives, puffing up with pie in place of lost pride. They were forever misfits, too midwestern to slip into whatever ironies or grace Connecticut had to offer. They yearned over the neighbor's fence ("just look at it," they would say, "just look at it") and I, embarrassed for them, would run off to swim the muddy river as if I could make myself into a skinny river rat smelling of boat oil and gasoline, unformed and free.

She called me into the darkened corner of her bedroom to ask help getting into her girdle. She stood on one foot at the edge of her closet with one piece over one thigh and pulled; she wanted me to pull at the other side once she got her other leg into position. I made a vow, but in those days I was always making impossible vows.

Raw eggs

There is a story that Robert Frost pretended to down three raw eggs before going on. It's hard to believe things if they don't happen to you. What's hardest to get is anyone else's experience, especially in America where experience, unregulated by custom or culture, counts for so much. If Joe says he wants to ride roller coasters for his fiftieth birthday, I have to forget the Ohio State Fair before polio and puberty when my father rocked me on the ferris wheel until I begged screaming for him to stop.

I ate raw eggs once when I was a teenager and was trying to get myself initiated into a high school sorority. I also put molasses and oats in my hair. So much groupiness, however, made me ill and I quit. For all of his affairs, Frost seems to have been a loner. I remember the quitting; what I can't get hold of is the original impulse, an experience that was mine and mine alone.

Trout

If the novel is dead, if the story. If fireflies caught in glass jars; if the jars filled with bread and butter pickles. Faith who made them the way her mother made them and who lives in the house she was born in on North Hill in Vermont broke her ankle. If the jar filled with grasses was a jar filled with popcorn which was the only thing I could eat during periods of high anxiety or the only thing to have for dinner when I'm consumed with self-pity or the only thing to have after swimming in the Ohio pool all morning, all afternoon, all day. My sisters and I came home in the chlorine-muggy late day, our fingers wrinkled and our lips blue, huddled under wet towels which we spread on the blacktop to dry and went in to make as much with butter and salt as we could get away with before dinner, and lay out on the towels eating it and sucking our fingers—our own, each other's—until we had all stuck together: towel to driveway, swimming suit to towel, hair to ears, cheek to jowl. If the umbilical cord is cut and words float like I learned to do first, head down, staring into the blue where there were no fish, no seaweed, no coral, no mud. In La Paz once, when I was still young enough to think things that happened to me would happen again, I snorkeled up against rainbow fish and looked in their eyes. Last Tuesday I was served a fresh trout from the San Gabriel Mountains; it had eyes as white and glazed as pus. I left the table to reread (O Dorothea) *Middlemarch*.

Artichokes

One evening a quite frantic and elegant Italian said he would make a beautiful artichoke salad. He couldn't make coffee; he couldn't sit still; he couldn't stay in one city for more than a week; he only lived in furnished rooms with matching drapes and paintings by the numbers. Nevertheless, he said, he knew how to make this one dish, no cooking, just cutting and marinating. At the end of it, there were mounds of leaves as he only needed the heart; and there were mounds of lemon skins as he only needed the juice. And there was a failed salad. These were American artichokes, not the artichokes he was familiar with and they were tough, stringy, recalcitrant, and bitter.

Everyone tells me translation is difficult. I am so American I really don't really know. What would I do without translation though in the midst of an argument in which one is presenting one's side can one ask the translator who disagrees to present one's views to the foreign guests?

What I do while traveling is what I do anyway, tune out in relief. I don't worry about having to do anything but get from here to there. One word seems enough: *speissig* is what he tells me describes the rubberband like device with the plastic *smetterling* to hold the bit of sponge in front of the spout of the teapot. The culture seems to come into focus. The elegant Italian also drinks tea and he made some after the salad failed and stayed with us for days during which we talked of Wallace Stevens but cooked and ate almost nothing. It was a great relief.

Adagia: Poetry is a pheasant disappearing in the brush.

Oatmeal

The most forgiving food is oatmeal. I eat it when I can't forgive myself or ones I most want to. Who do you think you are anyway, I think, who's going to make me, why should I? And why do I have to forgive someone for turning on me who can't think of how to keep anyone from turning angry of course the world is unjust and unfair. Peas Porridge cold and 9 days old.

John Berryman's image for guilt: *a grave Sienese face a thousand years/ would fail to blur the still profiled reproach of.*

Waking, I'm sure I dreamed a dream of forgiveness, although how I could have dreamed pictures so abstract and ineffable I'm not sure. I'm only sure that the whole night spent itself spilling over a sort of twilight from which I wake knowing that I dreamed of not being able to imagine any coherent system which would allow such an occurrence to happen, even if I were willing, which the lethargy of the dream, its weight and pull, demonstrates I am not. The pain inflicted is so specific and thorny. The sentence spoken in anger won't break up and dissipate. I make it with too much water so it is gooey and slippery. I hope it will do its stuff. I hear another's footsteps. I blow. I bite my tongue.

Cauliflower

In Vermont I had a chance at fresh vegetables from the garden everyday. It was August and the time for cauliflower everyday: steamed, stirfried, with pasta, cold with vinaigrette, raw, grilled. There was no way to keep up; the cauliflower grew to the size of basketballs and turned that "gone" color. One of us thought to blanch the heads to stop the enzymes, to dip them in a bucket of cold water, to bag them up, to freeze them for February; one of us said let's eat in season, in February we'll have turnips.

I reread books of poetry I had left behind last summer, books in which imagery is as specific as turnip. Why does vocabulary shift from west coast to east? I made lists of where poets lived; I thought of exceptions; I retraced my steps. Where I live abstraction envelopes us all like the air; Angelenos have a theory about everything. I thought about the way in which after several weeks in Vermont I feel a drag towards specific story, anecdote: Freddie's shack has been condemned by the state—it's without water, electricity, floor—and he's had to get out. He walks the five miles from town where he's been put up at the inn to the top of the hill where he's farmed for fifty years. He talks to his cows. He rakes hay off the slope by hand; you can't trust a tractor he says.

Basil

In California the potted basil blooms till Christmas. Gardens spring up under the freeways and feed families who have planted there since before they were built. The sun keeps on until no one can stand it. Those who can't stand to get old buy wet suits; a man we call "fishboy" has wrinkled fingers, smooth skin. He surfs each morning before going to work. Once I taught a student who sat in the front row, hair blown back in sticky peaks, his face scorched from the sun, his eyes an eerie blue. He tried to focus but was somewhere else, out of sync. The tape in the car has melted its music. We speak of oranges or tangerines we used to get for Christmas; such luxury is no longer a miracle since there are no seasons, no ages of man. It turns out carbon monoxide is good for plants.

Steak

A stand in for a missing communality. We've given up on politics, most of us, and religion hardly comes up. I have one friend who tries to bind the world together partly by the serious endeavor of faith, partly by metaphor. She goes to as many gatherings of as many different people as she can wearing clothes suitable for any occasion. I, on the other hand, want to change for every change in weather and mood. I dissolve in confusion trying to decide. But she gets dressed, indeed dressed up, in the morning and stays that way long into the night. It looks exhausting, even futile, but it's her calling. Mostly what we've got is the shared community of the movies; someone else can mimic the Duke: "If this is a shine, Rosie, I'm gonna hafta come back and iron your face." Others utter the same sentence in chorus and turn on their heels: I hate *It's a wonderful life*. Buddies under the skin.

My brother-in-law tries steak. He hopes it will please most of us and at the very least cause the rest of us to reminisce about family reunions and barbecues of yore. We'll be joined at the feet by the spirit of summers past, like Dickens' manacled ghost. Last time, though, as the family was sorting through done and well done and rare and raw and none ("I'm a vegetarian," she says) and only a small sliver please—each asserting preferences as tyrannical as ordering coffee—it was all too much for him; he couldn't hold it in and sprayed a mouthful of wine over the whole table. We were all bathed in one unifying red stain.

Coca Cola

Modern poetry is focused, they say, on the city; I know I am postmodern. We live, as Sarduy says, in schemata not sounds: *In Rome the sound of fountains can guide us through the maze of narrow streets; in Havana, the smell of the ocean... but only arrows and hypergraphic panels will guide us through the cloverleaf of highways superimposed on Stockholm.*

Or my city, L.A. I used to think we were all influenced in our writing by the cities we lived in, but I think now that we have all withdrawn and that the demise of language has to do not only with gangs and guns but also with abstraction: the city as arbitrary sign system. We don't go out.

In a BBC film I saw on Ezra Pound, I was amazed by the numbers of people milling around on the street, by crowds, by frayed elbows, by Poe's story about the man in the crowd, by Baudelaire's Paris, by the thump of contact. Today it's hard to get anyone to go anywhere but the movies: dark, safe, sensual in an abstract sort of way, like coke. I know people who used to go everywhere, now watch TV every night. There is no city left, only threat and direction signs. "Stop," they say, or "go."

Red pepper strips

Collage is a way of organizing *The Wasteland* among other things. Seemingly serendipitous panache.

A bit of memory (what I was once, what I ate once) embedded in a long poem: "I sat upon the shore/ Fishing."

I only like fragments which aren't. Beauty in presentation. Minimal bits of this or that, metallic.

What I liked about it was the strip of red pepper so thin you couldn't make out the taste before it dissolved. The word "jou" about to disappear before the jouissance of getting it—"rnal."

A strip of glue licked from a card I was making for Christmas and the sparkles that finally tarnished like real silver.

At the Japanese restaurant the long porcelain dish is so finely glazed that the silver scales of fish float on a green sea.

Rice

Gertrude Stein says it is hard living down the tempers we are born with. She sat for hers, writing all night, posing for Picasso. I bump into walls. Children shouldn't eat so many sweets they say. They say that if we would consume more grains we'd calm down. My kungfu master says I could have acupuncture to relieve fear of flying; or he says, try hypnosis, try homeopathy. Others among us are giving up eating altogether, becoming anorexics way into middle age. It happens to men. It happens to women. One gains self control and stands on her head. My favorite stories as a child were of Mrs. Pigglewiggle who could get bad children to shape up. In one she plants radish seeds in the dirty skin of a boy who won't take a bath. It was hard to sit still in the fourth grade and still is. I broke off the ends of crayons, ripped the edges off paper, pulled threads from hems. I tore kleenex in pieces and scattered them around my feet; I chewed my hair. If the world is unraveling, focus in. The world's in a grain of rice.

Snails

William Carlos Williams: *Because snails are slimy when alive and because slime is associated (erroneously) with filth, the fool is convinced that snails are detestable when, as it is proven every day, fried in butter with chopped parsley upon them, they are delicious.*

At some point one just fails. I made lots of mistakes growing up, more than my parents could keep track of, though they tried, and more than I could forgive myself for, given an idea of perfection we shared, but then came the time of my sister's graduation from high school when I was living in another city and in love with someone I couldn't introduce to my parents because I knew he would break my heart and knew they would know it and I wasn't ready yet for such knowledge which would mean I'd have to give up what I didn't want to.

We'd spent the day in New York, holing up for the afternoon in a hotel on Forty-second with rags for curtains, and ending up walking barefoot in parks I can't remember the names of and eating my first snails and drinking champagne at a bar near the train station. I arrived home late just as the family car was pulling out. My skirt was torn and dirty; my feet were so swollen I had to force them into my shoes. I reeked of garlic and drink. I was pushed into the backseat and driven to the graduation where I was made to sit alone in the backrow, a pariah and fool. Sex and the snails did me in. Small but deadly.

Tortillas

On a beach on an island off La Paz the best I've ever eaten made by the whore the fishermen brought for the day and for the night. They built her an umbrella of palm fronds to keep off the sun and went out for clams and she stood under the shade and moved her hands back and forth, back and forth, slapping. She smiled a gold-toothed smile. The man I was with knew the fishermen and all their children and cousins and neighbors at the cantina where the beer was warm and salty, the limes tart.

The motor died. I was frightened. I thought we might die on the island. No one knew we were there. I had a snail race with one of the boys who was the best diver but was tired. The sun beat down. We were tired of sleeping on thin blankets on the stony beach. We were tired of tortillas. In L.A. they are served under striped napkins like small blankets and when I see them I think of how I foolishly thought I would die a young and brilliant death or that I would see that sea again. Yesterday I tried to say to a young woman you can't just have an affair and step back into your life unchanged. No one gets the same river twice. The boy speared rainbow fish which turned immediately gray. No one was hungry. No one knew how to fix the motor. After many days the brother of one of the fishermen noticed we were missing from the cantina and came out and rescued us in a small boat with a motor that like my heart skipped beats.

Chocolate

There is a red flower that smells of chocolate; there is a woman smelling it though I haven't given it to her yet for her wedding which was months ago. There are roses in the stew for her bridal dinner. If my ears cave in; if you remembered my place in line. Everyone's lining up for something bright and chocolate. When the kid comes selling peanuts drenched in stale chocolate you can't resist sending him to college or camp or the opportunity of selling more magazines door to door. Chocolate is the hope of marriage in spring which Hamlet says no to. But who can slam the door everytime?

Baked potato

The best meals I've ever had have been in the face of actual hunger. I like best to come in from the cold or wet and eat a baked potato. I like it, a single mound on a plate, brown and wrinkled. I like the smell of it, the difference between the texture of the pulp and the texture of the slight gritty taste of the skin, and butter and salt. Some Indian cultures are suspicious of salt because it is eating earth. I like that no one has done anything to it.

It remains boggling to me how much revision is necessary, not to everyone—one writer I know says she never does. But whatever I write that I like comes with doing it over again. All the first things are lumpish. I saw a poem once that seems to me to have been mostly white space—some poets are rhapsodic about white space—and some few nouns: rock, cloud, tree. Not the Carson McCullers story about the old man at the bar telling the boy that love fails because men start at the wrong end, at the climax, and fall in love with women.

The old man reached over and grasped the boy by the collar of his leather jacket. He gave him a gentle little shake and his green eyes gazed down unblinking and grave. "Son, do you know how love should be begun?" The boy sat small and listening and still. Slowly he shook his head. The old man leaned closer and whispered: "A tree. A rock. A cloud."

Piecrust

Sing a song of sixpence, a pocket full of rye; four and twenty blackbirds baked in a pie.

The blackbird whirled in the autumn winds.
It was a small part of the pantomime.

—WALLACE STEVENS

I know one cook well. I've known him all my life it seems. He makes apple pies with crosshatched slivers of crust; in the corners there are veined leaves cut from dough. It's an arbor to eat. There are seven birds sitting on the telephone wire and they are screaming. What they are screaming is unclear to the man who is sitting across from me in his armchair positioned at an angle to the window from which he can see some percentage of the grouping. Although he has been asleep for several hours he is now awake and his face is turned more or less towards the window. The curtains which his wife put up more than ten years ago are slightly parted. The plaid of the material picks up the crosshatch pattern of the windowframe. Now he pads in his slippers into the kitchen and eats the pie he wishes were there.

Cheese and crackers

William Carlos Williams: *The raw beauty of ignorance that lies like an opal mist over the west coast of the Atlantic, beginning at the Grand Banks and extending into the recesses of our brains—the children, the married, the unmarried—clings especially about the eyes and the throats of our girls and boys.*

I was walking after dinner —actually we'd just had cheese and crackers because we'd had lunch out at the Steak and Ale and no one was hungry but you have to eat something before going to bed, my aunt says, because she says at 86 you can't sleep if you don't eat something. In Florida the streets connect directly to the sky which is, from my point of view, the only real reason for Florida.

Everyone who's out walking looks like a lonely stick against the pale streets and sky. There were three of us walking towards the condos on the golf course and three boys playing basketball on a neighbor's drive. The men were swollen and red-faced, fathers with new vans in the carports, making their ways dizzily across vacant lots. Were they trying to walk out of their lives?

Were they drunk as they looked? What were they doing there in so much emptiness before or after dinner as if they were wanting to walk towards something which might once have been the center of town and which now was, simply and unforgivingly, sky.

Rappini

Rappini calls up Rapunzel and wandering about in a garden at night by starlight ravenous for greens. The witch was promised the unborn child. It is hard to let loose of these stories. They keep one pinned to beds. They drift in and out. Sheets are flying everywhere. The desire and fear of turning into the opposite sex. Witches are both, boil, boil, toil and trouble with breasts and beards, fingers and toes. Being trapped in a tower and hanging out long braids of blond hair: Rapunzel, Rapunzel, let down your golden hair.

These days I want to sleep forever as if by that I could understand age. Now I think I am still a boy of eight playing baseball. Now I am old, not suddenly, of course, but inexplicably and for sure. Rappini is flaccid and delicious as how hard it would be to invent the color green if one had never seen it. It looks like two different things, a bit of collard green and a bit of broccoli. Some people believe that food is food and they can compare one sort with another and remember ingredients. Cookbooks seem to me as preposterous as poetry, the imaginative leap as great. Each meal is as if one found oneself wandering barefoot in a garden in the dark.

Coffee

I have measured out my life with coffee spoons.

Coffee measures both time and style.

Sunflower seeds

Eating sunflower seeds driving the dark country road to hear poets read at Bennington College in summer. I confess to eating very well in between these jaunts, but nothing's so good as stealth, chips or seed spilling between hands and knees. Solipsism and the forbidden on the highway. As a child I was forbidden to eat in the car. What seems almost impossible now is that time was then so precisely divided up. Events didn't collide. Sociologists tell us we slide from table to den and TV is the hearth. We eat on the run. Free verse is speaking to us across the airwaves. Whitman cries along the highways.

> *The smoke of my own breath,*
> *Echoes, ripples, buzz'd whispers, love-root, silk-thread,*
> *   crotch and vine,*
> *My respiration and inspiration, the beating of my heart,*
> *   the passing of blood and air through my lungs.*

I like tossing the seeds around. I like the air from the open window. I too like heavy breathing. There is noth-

ing to wipe up and no guilt to speak of and on these
roads even the radio doesn't come in.

Diet shakes

Simone Weil: *It may be that vice, depravity and crime are nearly always...attempts to eat beauty, to eat what we should only look at.*

I always wanted dinner in colored pills. I thought it would be as beautiful as Lake Erie at sunset. The feet of men stepping into the lake at sunset. The rings on the water like flat colored pills, one after another, after another. Catherine of Siena ate only the host flat and white and singularly beautiful. But saintliness isn't what I was looking for. When they wade into the water and disappear.

Horseradish

Once I phoned my son in his first apartment; there was nothing in the refrigerator; he said he was having a condiment sandwich. My nephew likes gobs of ketchup on everything; his mother says, enough. My mother liked horseradish. It brought tears to her eyes. It reminded her of home. Once she sat on the stairs with a college friend of mine and talked as people talk on stairs. She talked as if she were my age or no age and didn't have to be the mother she returned to when she went back down stairs. Tears came to her eyes about something I can't remember; she had had a recurrent dream about losing a child. What does it mean, she asked, as if I could tell her. She joined the flower club when she found everyone turning to her for advice. She didn't have a clue she said and turned to roses.

Something in the water
    like a flower
    will devour
    water
    flower (Lorine Niedecker)

Bananas

In search of perfection and what you can carry in one hand I take bananas. That way I never have to think about lunch. I hate thinking about lunch and if I had it my way I could eat all three meals at once and have it over and done with. I'd never have to break my stride but could keep on. Thoreau thought that if he walked long enough he would get to heaven.

In his "Fifth Walk" Rousseau says, *Nothing keeps the same unchanging shape, and our affections, being attached to things outside us, necessarily change and pass away as they do. Always out ahead of us or lagging behind, they recall a past which is gone or anticipate a future which may never come into being.*

Like many Americans my eye is not on the ball. I don't like bananas cut up in a fruit salad because they turn brown and fruit salads are overrated as they are always excuses for something else, but a whole banana is perfect and reminds one both of where one has been and of where one is going. I do think most Americans are off register, thinking not exactly about the life to come, but something like it—which is why there is so much rushing about and why I tend to get lost and why Americans are not really materialists.

I once sat with my father on a wall overlooking Long Island Sound at twilight and saw that despite the beauty of it all he had set his jaw again and would have, as I now have, a headache in the morning when he woke up. I wanted to say, what more could anyone want, but I asked him instead what he had wanted in life and he said he had wanted to earn a million dollars but hadn't. He got up and walked through the sliding glass doors to look for the perfect martini.

Eggs

Overlap grows stronger as one grows older. A single egg has an egg behind it and behind it an egg. Each scene, even the most neutral, hatches ones from before. There is sun coming out from behind the rain. I no longer eat scrambled eggs for breakfast but omelettes for dinner. On Sunday mornings my father got to sleep in while we went to church in clothes laid out the night before no matter how many people had trooped in, how much liquor, how many cigarettes. Someone could always play the piano and someone could belt out a song like Ethel Merman. After one Ohio State football game and after three hours of sleep, grown men played what looked to be a game of hot potato football in the attic where they'd slept.

After we got home I was to make scrambled eggs for my father who sat alone and silent in his pajamas at the table while I brought the plate and cleared it away. What worried me was that the butter kept turning brown as it melted and then the eggs would be brown and though he ate them I knew they weren't right.

It is a photograph in multiples this man in pajamas sitting so still. Reproduced again and again his face sags and his beard turns gray. Camera imitates memory as the same image comes up slightly watery, slightly bent. He never spoke as I served and washed up. Mother said he worked hard for us all week and did I understand. What resentment I felt then seems as resentment does at such a distance, shrunken and shrinking as in mirrored images the figure grows smaller and smaller. Our clothes matched; navy blue coats and broad brimmed hats with ribbons. "Keep up the good work" floats its caption over the table in the kitchen with the man eating his eggs.

Toast and ghosts

Perhaps it's the ghosts fill me up. The potent one fades now I am twice as old, but still comes each summer in dreams, his skin smelling of butter and toast. Long dead, he's the future, and when he's around I see a lavender haze that kept me in my twenties from being only anxious and dogged, his solid body an inexplicable comfort to me. Once we drove along the Merritt Parkway in a sudden snowstorm; the road was icy and cars were skidding out all around. I fell asleep in complete assurance as never before or since. For three hours I am convinced I was shifted into the body of someone else so I would know what it was like.

My mother hangs over backyards in an aqua dress as if she were a saint returned for some purpose. It hasn't yet been revealed. I am surprised by her Romanesque feet hanging down, bony and elongated, and that she's wearing a color she never liked at all. My grandmother came out of the closet after her funeral and asked why I was sleeping in her bed. She wanted to know if I were picking at the threads in her down comforter.

She doesn't like comic books in bed. When she isn't looking, I brush the crumbs to the floor.

Pizza and ghosts

I was a single mother for years. Then we hit puberty and were possessed. One year I battled with my teenage son so madly that I fell down stairs and banged into doorways. I threatened, blew up, and begged. In the summer we separated for two weeks and one night during those weeks I woke in the night to a grotesque face in the corner shadows, limbs and legs, arms and feet dangling from the great mouth chewing and swallowing. I ran to my neighbor who explained I had had an hallucination. Yes, I said, madly, but what, I know it, I do. He said, it is Goya's etching of Cronos eating his own children.

My son came home; I came home. The ghastly fury passed out and away from us. We put on Bach fugues, our mutual music of reconciliation, and sent out for pizza.

Plum sauce

He says there was phosphorescence on the road to the cabin the first summer you came here, do you remember. I don't but say I do. I'm getting to an age where I remember vaguely, where dreams I have, the knee of a man I hardly know, the baby I blow life into after flattening him in my sleep, the murdering violinist, are as vivid as coffee. A gnat floats on the top. The life I don't lead is as demanding as the one I do. I worry about what to say or wear in scenes I'll never know. The deadman glows in the dark. I don't believe the friends I wash dishes for believe I am standing in their kitchen. I have lied so long and stood so apart from my life, I can't think of why not. I gravitate towards those who speak with absolute certainty: the Marxist, the human rights activist, the one who says no.

He says it ought to get into a poem and I'm sure he's right. On the Cape once four people went swimming at night, sex in the air and phosphorescent jelly fish in the black waves. All of them hurt each other, not just once but time and again as if betrayal were an intricate and aesthetic form. The air was soft. Later I walked with the husband of the other woman in an Arboretum just as petals were falling all around. Why does this scene come back to me again and again as if it were, as it wasn't, momentous. Or perhaps lilacs don't scatter and it's the frizzled white poppy here I'm thinking of as it tosses its head to the stone path defiantly and all at once.

How does the cook whose dishes I wash know to put plum in a sauce for chicken and gives me the recipe I put in a drawer and never take out. What I like about weather, what I miss often in California, is that it chooses you. You have to wear a coat.

Zucchini and mint

The thing about the table is there is so much going on. I can never figure out how people find it in their hearts to eat. To get something by heart. Medieval people thought it, not the mind, the seat of memory. There are arguments about politics, frets over children, egos in a tangle, plates to be cleared and a pale boy pointedly mute. Not to mention the heart and love. I mutter foreign phrases under my breath as if I could speak another tongue.

People turn transparent. I feel at the dinner hour as if you can see directly into those sitting across the table. The guests are blown glass figurines for sale on Olvera Street, twisted and fragile: a dragon with wings, a horse, a ballerina on point. Servings seem grotesque. Someone says autism is defined by not being able to stand the slightest rearrangement of the room. At the other end someone says how can you say that. Someone says, you fool. I wash dishes when I'm supposed to be eating and sing old hymns about apes swinging to and fro. I think I ought to be able to shape an evening as the glassblower his dragon, out to pass around ease as well as zucchini with mint which everyone says is like a weed but for me keeps turning brown.

Should an evening have shape, moral, aesthetic, or otherwise. The cook says a person must be a monument, a piece of work, a force, or he's nothing at all. Yelling has a shape of its own. I like standing at the sink afterwards when the shape of an evening seems clear and begins to arrange itself again along the limbs. The pedals break off the piano and the violinist, so much given over to her sonata, breaks down, quivers, and can't go on.

Cottage cheese and brandy

Want is a state not only of mind. I've never been hungry. The closest I came was the result of a poverty inflicted by my own desire to study and not to borrow. It was artificial because I knew it would end, because I was too pretentious to want for much, and because I had friends who would tide me over if it came to that. I read late and early, on the bus, in bed, in the tub, all night, the pages bent and soggy, pen marks on the sheets and cheeks. I ate cottage cheese and drank cheap brandy to get to sleep after a day in which I took on all the symptoms of the patients wandering the psychiatric ward of the hospital where I worked.

One knows some things only as a voyeur. I look back on that young woman obsessed and certain, who scrubbed the three steps between the front room and the street as if it would ward off what had already happened. She resists intrusion. I look at her and can't understand how she thought she was Spenser's heroic Britomart, why she imagined she was making any sort of dent, what kept her blinded to what was obvious and all around. She is as foreign to me as the images haunting those other eyes. Their eyes and what might be behind them took away all appetite until at the end of the summer I drank a bottle of brandy and could never stomach it again.

Plums

I have eaten
the plums
that were in
the icebox

You are never straightforward he says after she tells
him how much she likes M because M is so straightforward.

She clarifies, I don't mean sincere.

He says it's because you had a close relationship with
your mother.

She says M took so many drugs she had to back up to
ground zero.

He says you probably don't even know what you mean
most of the time. He gives me another example. The
specific is tricky. It seems to locate truth and many get
fooled.

There are many place names and places on a body and specific moments in specific poems and even specific parodies of specific moments in specific poems. She's off to walk barefoot on the singing beach. Yesterday the girl who was visiting with her parents said I have to dust between my toes. She'd wear pink tulle and marching pink pearl earrings. Wouldn't she? Didn't she? A dancer from France is what she wanted to be. He'd say, straightforward is what you are and thanks for the plums.

Mushrooms

Sometimes people say what do you want for dinner.
They say this early in the morning right after breakfast. Others say what they would like or what they will
buy at the store or what has come up in the garden or
what restaurant they would like to go to. I hit a wall;
my mind's a blank, perspiration forms and I can't think
of a thing. I can hardly remember what food is or what
it might be at seven or eight PM or what it might be to
bring fork to mouth. "Who are you" was said to Alice
from the top of a tall mushroom. I can't seem to plan
and don't believe in the future. Couldn't it just arrive
on time, perfectly formed, without the fuss and bother
of going to the supermarket?

Inspiration could be like that but years ago I came to
terms with the fact that inspiration needs working at.
You have to sit there for a given period of time. One
writer I know says that good writing mainly requires
a good seat. Everyone struggles with the will which is
sometimes, oddly, its opposite, a sort of Keatsian help-
lessness one works to wait for. My favorite way with a
mushroom is to put a Portabello in an old iron skillet

with olive oil and garlic and you can also sprinkle it with balsamic and soy sauce and add salt and pepper and then you press it flatter with another iron skillet and then it is done and you slice it up and eat it. It is hard to imagine there could be such a thing as a mushroom. In pictures they look underwater dangerous as they are. What was it Alice said?

Summer squash

Giving things up is a great temptation. Many seem to do it for moral reasons; mostly I have none. I like rooms free of clutter and bare walls that catch patterns of light and one stem of bamboo striped as a summer squash in a chartreuse vase. Almost anything green. Renunciation sometimes simply happens, not a choice but an imposition. A character in a novel says, "I simply do what I can so that things renounce me."

I used to think that museums of the future would offer blank walls for those suffering sensory overload, for the overwrought and stressed out. The paintings would all be crated and put in storage and we'd visit for the rare occasion of white walls and silence. The curator would mark the floor with x's to show where to stand. The pattern of the people, the absence of the man meant to be at x14 or the presence of two at x3 would take total concentration. Her dress would be of green linen, long and handmade; the seams never lie flat, the selvages too wide. The gaps between notes in a Cage piece would expand. He'd leave his cello behind.

I like the same thing for breakfast, the same thing for lunch, ditto for dinner. During one period I ate only rice and stirfried summer squash with chopsticks in a bowl, a green failure from a local pottery. In Japan the rooms were bare but for tatami and rice-paper paneled cupboard doors; the bedding was folded up for the day and put away. In the class on the tea ceremony, more arcane than other versions, already arcane, the transition from one section to the next was signaled by the faint click of the wooden server as it was dropped from a height of two inches against a small stone.

The last entry in MFK Fisher's *Last House*: *Missing must be accepted as part of any thinking existence, and made use of. It is a force.*

Champagne risotto

Afterwards N always calls to say what he thought of
the dinner.
It was a strange sort of evening he says.
He says who else's invited and are you ok.
Or something about someone he can't stand.
He asks how are you again.
I say I'll tell you later.
He says there wasn't enough or too much.

At the accident the witness said she had run the light
and the other witness said she'd stopped in time. The
police wrote it all down and filed a report.

He says you have to use champagne.
He says who was that woman who kept to herself and
why.
What are you going to do about your life he says.
He says something wicked and don't mind me.
Everyone has to read Turgenev.
He hangs up before I tell him how I am.
I am grateful for that.

Parsley

The table's set. The glasses toss light around. The lily has too strong a fragrance and we take it away. The napkins are folded under the fork; the napkins are folded to the left of the fork; the napkins are paper and linen and towel. Someone says there must be music and disappears to find some. Someone says it is no good to have background music if the music is serious and who wants any other kind. The dishes are new, from antique stores, chips on the edges or stamps on the bottom or belonged to a mother.

I had an argument years ago that was partly serious and partly frivolous but necessary, and we were stuck in it and in the small airless apartment we'd rented in August. I'd mopped the floor for the umpteenth time but it had done no good. In the kitchen closet under the eaves we found on old set and decided to break them as if we were characters in a novel. I threw them against the wall. The wall broke and plaster came down as dust on the still intact plates.

Yesterday is a concept like folding and unfolding. Yesterday I ironed the table cloth. It crisscrosses the table. I read that they always invited him, but sometimes he came and sometimes he didn't and then the hostess died and he mourned his lover who either had or hadn't committed suicide, all the more. The lily announces itself and the table it is in the middle of and the history of western painting. There is wine but he drinks only beer or takes a sip and moves to water or refuses any. The girlfriend eats only eggs this week and next week only meat and not bread; she knows he is leaving her. Soon it's over and everyone has gone home and the smells of the cooking begin to rise and permeate the rooms and drapes and the *ordori* for the soup has just been stirred and the slow blending occurs as time moves backwards and the car in reverse at the store they have no more parsley and there is none in the garden though I recommend the Italian kind with its flat, hand-like leaves that looks like cilantro but is decidedly different.

GREEN INTEGER
Pataphysics and Pedantry

Edited by Per Bregne
Douglas Messerli, *Publisher*
Essays, Manifestos, Statements, Speeches, Maxims,
Epistles, Diaristic Notes, Narratives, Natural Histories,
Poems, Plays, Performances, Ramblings, Revelations
and all such ephemera as may appear necessary
to bring society into a slight tremolo of confusion
and fright at least.

*

Green Integer Books

Drifting Dominic Cheung [2000]
Victoria Knut Hamsun [2000]

Green Integer EL-E-PHANT books:

The PIP Anthology of World Poetry of the 20th Century, Volume 1
Douglas Messerli, editor [2000]
readiness / enough / depends / on Larry Eigner [2000]

BOOKS FORTHCOMING FROM GREEN INTEGER

Islands and Other Essays Jean Grenier
Operatics Michel Leiris
The Doll and *The Doll at Play* Hans Bellmer
[with poetry by Paul Éluard]
Water from a Bucket Charles Henri Ford
Suicide Circus: Selected Poems Alexei Kruchenykh
American Notes Charles Dickens
To Do: A Book of Alphabets and Birthdays Gertrude Stein
Prefaces and Essays on Poetry William Wordsworth
Licorice Chronicles Ted Greenwald
The Complete Warhol Screenplays I Ronald Tavel
Confessions of an English Opium-Eater Thomas De Quincey
The Renaissance Walter Pater
Venusburg Anthony Powell
Captain Nemo's Library Per Olav Enquist
Against Nature J. K. Huysmans
Partial Portraits Henry James

Utah Toby Olson
Rosa Knut Hamsun
The Pretext Rae Armantrout
Selected Poems and Journal Fragments Maurice Gilliams
Pedra Canga Tereza Albues